Made in United States
North Haven, CT
11 May 2024

52405646R00065